W9-DBZ-185

My Very Own Horse Book

by *Cornelia Thompson*

KLUTZ

KLUTZ is a kid's company staffed entirely by real human beings. We began our corporate life in 1977 in an office we shared with a Chevy Impala. Today we've outgrown our founding garage, but Palo Alto, California, remains Klutz galactic headquarters. For those of you who collect corporate mission statements, here's ours:

Create Wonderful Things
Be Good
Have Fun

Write Us.
We would love to hear your comments regarding this or any of our books. We have many!

KLUTZ.
450 Lambert Avenue
Palo Alto, CA 94306

Book printed in China.
Horse, box, leather, ribbon, blanket clips and girth strap with buckle manufactured in China. All other parts manufactured in Taiwan.

©2006 Klutz. All rights reserved.
Published by Klutz, a subsidiary of Scholastic Inc. Scholastic and associated logos are trademarks and/or registered trademarks of Scholastic Inc. Klutz and associated logos are trademarks and/or registered trademarks of Klutz.

Distributed in the UK by Scholastic UK Ltd
Westfield Road, Southam, Warwickshire
CV47 0RA   England

Distributed in Australia by
Scholastic Australia Customer Service
PO Box 579, Gosford NSW 2250
Australia

ISBN 1-57054-845-5
4 1 5 8 5 7 0 8 8 8

KLUTZ.com
Come on in!

OPEN 24 HOURS

Visit Our Website
You can check out all the stuff we make, find a nearby retailer, request a catalog, sign up for a newsletter, e-mail us or just goof off!

CONTENTS

Are you Horse Crazy?

True or False

☐ I own at least one model horse.

☐ The smell of a horse makes my knees weak.

☐ I'd rather muck out a stall than clean my room.

☐ I own at least three books about horses.

☐ I have accidentally referred to my locker as a stall.

☐ I doodle horses in class.

☐ I have, or have had, an imaginary horse.

☐ I would rather attend a horse show than a school dance.

☐ I can describe what a bay looks like.

☐ I suspect I whinny in my sleep.

☐ I have gone window shopping for horses on the internet.

☐ I have secretly pretended that my bicycle is a horse.

How many did you mark true?

1: Try again

2–5: Mild fever

6–9: High fever

10–11: Delirium

All 12: You are certifiably horse crazy. There is no hope for you.

Horse fever is far more common than the common cold. It can start with your first reading of *Black Beauty* or your first sighting of a mounted police officer in the heart of a city — and from there the affliction can run wonderfully rampant throughout your entire life. Once the bug hits, you'll experience cravings for information, pictures, stories and opportunities to be around horses whether you own your own or not. *My Very Own Horse Book* fulfills some of those cravings with solid, basic horse information *and* your own family-approved, house-friendly, low-maintenance horse. Take him out of his stall and refer to him as you read this book. If you are supremely lucky enough to have your own real live horse, you can refer to him or her, too.

5

What makes a horse a horse?

Horses are equines. They belong to the genus *equus* along with zebras, mules and donkeys.

The first thing to understand about equines is that they are prey animals. This colors the way they think and how they react to the world around them.

All prey animals are highly sensitive to the sound, sight and smell of danger. They have the flight-or-fight instinct. Their primary defense is to flee, but they can be worthy fighters if cornered. This instinct to run first, along with the ability to run fast, keeps a horse alive in the wild.

What makes a horse run?

Perceived danger. To a horse, danger can be anything known or unknown, visible or invisible, real or imagined, if it is lurking someplace it wasn't the day before. Or something that has always been in the same place, only today it looks or smells suspicious.

In short, it's hard to always know what might make a horse nervous. That's why we have to learn to think like prey.

Prey vs. Predator

Prey animals, such as horses and deer, are hunted.

Prey animals are usually grazing animals that live in herds.

Prey animals have eyes on the sides of their heads. They can see almost 360 degrees around.

Prey animals have large ears to pick up sounds of approaching danger.

Although they can be fierce fighters, a prey animal's first line of defense is to run away. Fast.

Predators, such as wolves, lions and tigers, hunt.

Predators can live in groups and hunt either alone or in teams.

Predators have eyes on the front of their heads, allowing them to have keen depth perception as they focus on the object of their hunt.

Predators have sharp teeth and claws to bring down their prey.

Yes, humans count as predators.

What Your Horse Wants from YOU

There is safety in numbers. This is why horses desire alliances with other animals and humans. In a herd, the leader sets the tone for the group. This is where you come in. Your horse wants you to be the leader of your own two-member herd. Here are some pointers on becoming a good leader:

Learn all you can about horses. Read about them. Take classes and lessons. Find a good trainer and follow them around — take notes.

Spend time with a horse. Hang out with him in his stall or paddock. You'll be amazed at what you learn.

Think like a horse. Learn the difference between a horse who is misbehaving and one who is afraid or doesn't understand you.

Keep a regular routine for feeding, grooming and working your horse. They like predictability.

Touch them. Horses feel reassured by touch. Grooming your horse is a great bonding activity since grooming one another in the wild is how horses make friends.

Move quietly around them. Big movements or loud behavior can upset a horse.

Talk to them. Horses like the sound of company. Horses, even model horses, are excellent listeners so talking to them is good for us humans, too.

Be confident. Horses reflect the emotions around them. If you are fearful, they will get worried. If you are confident, they will walk through fire or jump the moon for you.

Horses will groom each other in the wild to make friends.

How to Build a Horse
and your horse vocabulary...

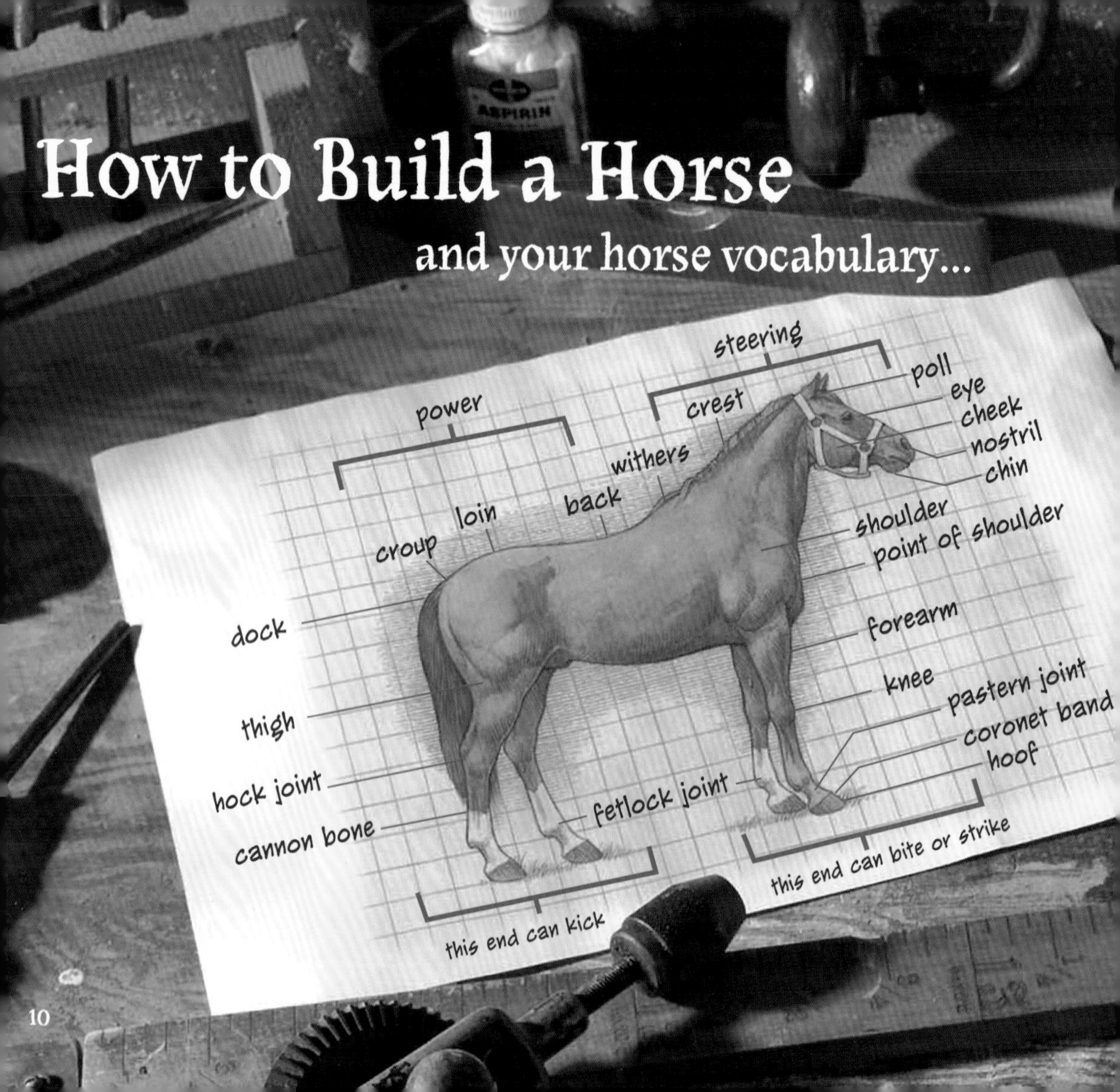

steering

power

crest

poll

eye

cheek

nostril

chin

withers

back

loin

croup

shoulder

point of shoulder

dock

forearm

thigh

knee

pastern joint

coronet band

hoof

hock joint

fetlock joint

cannon bone

this end can bite or strike

this end can kick

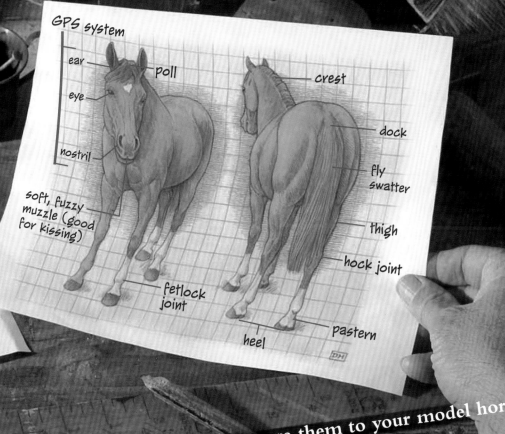

GPS system

ear — poll

crest

eye —

dock

fly swatter

nostril —

soft, fuzzy muzzle (good for kissing) —

thigh

hock joint

fetlock joint

pastern

heel

DH

Study these plans and compare them to your model horse.

Do horses have hands?

People are measured in feet and inches (or centimeters). Horses are measured in hands, from the ground to the top of their withers. A hand is equal to 4 inches (10.5 cm). To measure a horse, you can use a special measuring stick like the one in the photo. These sticks give you measurements in both hands and inches.

On average, a horse stands 15–16 hands at the withers and weighs 1100–1300 pounds (495–585 kg). Pony breeds are 14.2 hands or shorter.

TEETH

A mature horse has 36–40 teeth, none of which ever stop growing. As a horse ages, his teeth become longer and increasingly slanted outward. This is why you can tell a horse's age by looking at his teeth. In the wild, horses keep their teeth worn down through constant grazing, but in captivity they need the help of a horse dentist. These specialists will float (file down), any overgrown or sharp teeth.

LIPS

Horse lips can pick out the tastiest blades of grass. It's a great feeling to hold a piece of apple or carrot on the palm of your hand and let a horse gently pluck it up with such nimble lips! But always keep your hand flat, with your fingers together so he doesn't accidentally nibble on you!

NOSTRILS

Unlike humans or dogs, horses cannot breathe through their mouths. That's why those nostrils are so BIG.

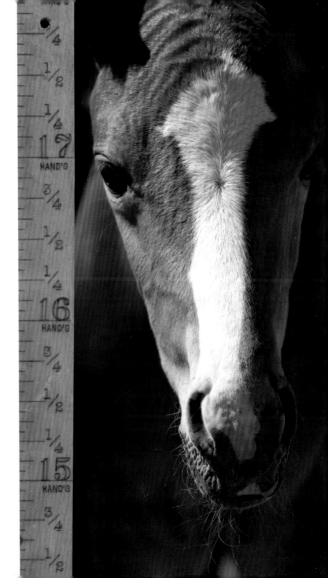

LEGS

Horses are born ready to run. When a foal is born, his legs are already 90 percent of the length they will be when he's full grown. Like many prey animals, foals can stand within an hour of birth. They can gallop within two hours.

HOOVES

In the wild, horses have tough hooves that stay trim from 20–30 miles (30–50 km) of grazing a day. But the feet of most domesticated horses are protected by iron or aluminum shoes. Every 6–8 weeks the shoes need to be pulled off and the hoof trimmed. Shoes are shaped to the horse's foot by a farrier (horseshoer) and then nailed into the wall of the hoof. Don't worry, it doesn't hurt! The wall of the hoof has no nerve endings.

Pick up your Klutz horse (don't try to pick up a real horse). Turn him over and look at the bottom of his feet. You'll see a little triangular-shaped area called the frog. The frog acts as a shock absorber and is the most sensitive part of the foot. When you clean out the hooves, you should be gentle around the frog.

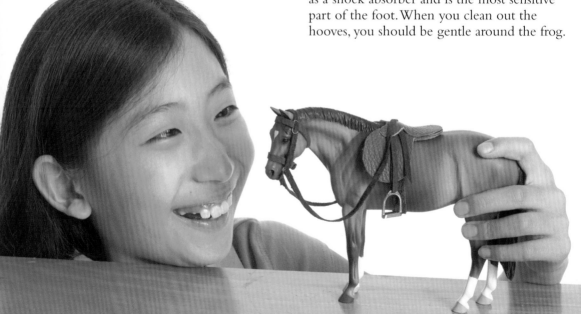

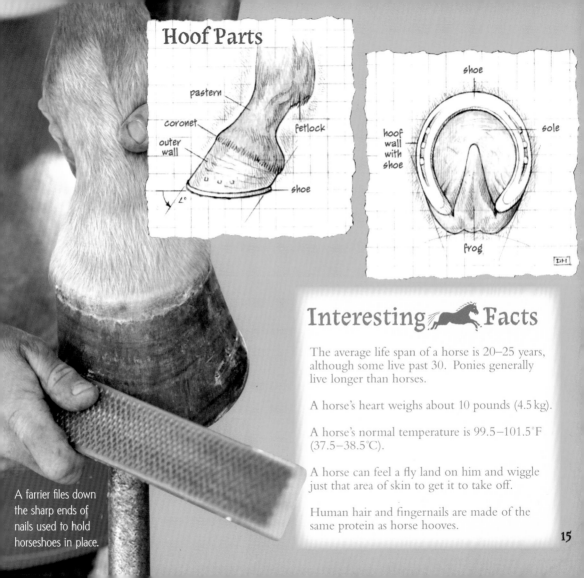

Hoof Parts

pastern

coronet

fetlock

outer wall

shoe

∠7°

shoe

hoof wall with shoe

sole

frog

DH

Interesting Facts

The average life span of a horse is 20–25 years, although some live past 30. Ponies generally live longer than horses.

A horse's heart weighs about 10 pounds (4.5 kg).

A horse's normal temperature is 99.5–101.5°F (37.5–38.5°C).

A horse can feel a fly land on him and wiggle just that area of skin to get it to take off.

Human hair and fingernails are made of the same protein as horse hooves.

A farrier files down the sharp ends of nails used to hold horseshoes in place.

15

Markings

One of the ways to describe a horse is by his markings — the coloration on his body, face and legs.

Here are some of the basic markings you'll come across in horses.

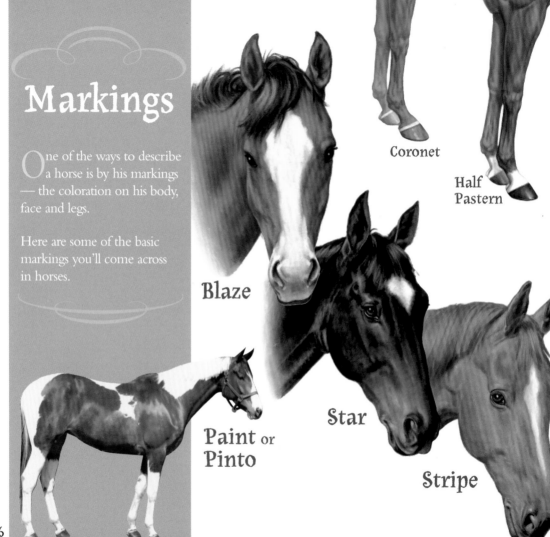

Coronet

Half Pastern

Blaze

Paint or Pinto

Star

Stripe

Sock

Stocking

Bald Face

Snip

Leopard Spots

colors

Horses come in countless color variations. Here are the classics.

CHESTNUT
coppery red color all over, including mane and tail

PAINT
colored body with large white patches or white body with large colored patches

BAY
brown or reddish-brown body with black points (lower legs, nose, mane and tail)

DAPPLED GRAY
white and black hairs mixed to make a gray appearance; gray horses start out dark-colored and whiten as they age

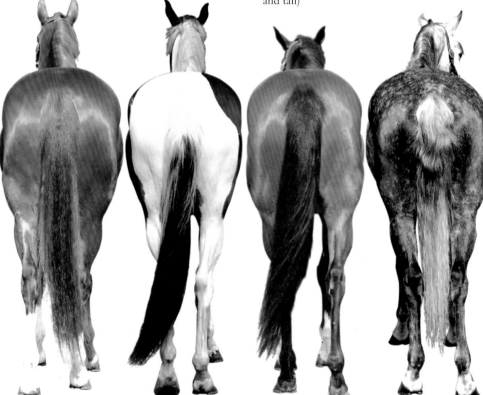

PALOMINO

golden body with blond mane and tail

BLACK

black all over, including mane and tail — no light-brown areas

SORREL

chestnut body with blond mane and tail

WHITE

Most white horses are actually very light gray. If you look closely, their skin is black. Truly white horses are albino, with pink eyes, hooves and skin.

BUCKSKIN

cream or golden body with black points; will often have a black stripe down the back

Horse to Human Dictionary

Although they don't use spoken or written language as we do, horses know how to get their messages across. If you listen with your eyes, you'll catch what a horse has to say: Horses use body language to let you know what they're thinking.

Ear Signals

A horse's ears tell you a lot. Here is a beginner's dictionary to their language.

Ears softly held and facing sideways:
The look of a happy relaxed horse.

"Life is good. Nothing scary is on the radar screen."

Ears up and facing forward:
This horse is zeroing in on something.

"Wow, that's interesting, but not scary... yet" or *"This is fun! I'm having a good time."*

Ears flat against the head so that they almost disappear: This is "pinning" the ears and is the look of a seriously grumpy horse.

"Back off buddy." (This can be followed by a kick or a bite — so take it seriously.)

Ears facing gently backward: This can mean he's concentrating on the messages he's getting from his rider.

"I'm listening to you. I'm concentrating on what you're saying to me." or "What's going on behind me?"

Ears flicking back and forth very quickly with head held high: This horse is trying to gather as much information as he can — fast.

"I'm really worried!" (His next move could be to turn and bolt— so pat him and speak soothingly to him. And hang on, just in case.)

Lip Language

Humans talk with their tongues and lips. Horses can, too. If a horse licks his lips and makes chewing motions with his mouth, it's a sign of trust and comfort.

"I'm no threat to you. And I know you are no threat to me."

Tail Talk

If a horse is annoyed or uncomfortable, he might switch his tail a lot — (as opposed to softly swishing it happily.) Tails also act as efficient fly swatters in the summer. If you enter a horse's stall and it turns its rump to you, this is not a good sign.

"You are not welcome here." (Don't argue. Get an experienced horseperson.)

Horse Noises

Neigh or Call:
"I'm over here! Where are you?"
This is a request for information, to find out where other horses are. It isn't an indication of fear or aggression.

Squeal:
"Ok that's enough small talk. Back off now." Squeals are directed at other horses, not at people. Horses will squeal at each other to put an end to a nose-sniffing session. Mares will squeal at stallions to flirt.

Nicker:
A lovely, low, staccato sound that says, "Hi there. I'm so happy to see you."
If you hang around at feeding time, you'll hear a lot of nickering. Horses will nicker to each other and to people.

Whinny:
"Hi! I'm REALLY glad to see you!"
Sort of a shortened version of the neigh or a lengthened version of the nicker. A more emphatic way to greet a horse or person.

Horse Terms

Stallion	male horse over 4 years
Colt	male horse under 4 years
Mare	female horse over 4 years
Filly	female horse under 4 years
Foal	baby horse
Sire	father of a horse
Dam	mother of a horse
Gelding	neutered male horse

Interesting Facts

The horse is the official state animal of New Jersey.

The official high jump record goes to Captain Alberton Larraguibel Morales on Huaso — 8'2" (2.5 m) in 1949.

The average gestation period for a horse is 11 months but anything between 10 and 12 months is considered normal.

Interesting  Fact

Horses need 10–15 gallons (38–57 liters) of water per day.

A horse's stomach can hold 9–10 quarts (8.5–9.5 liters) of food at any one time.

A 1200-pound (545.5 kg) horse can live on grass in the wild. A human would die if they tried to live on grass alone!

WHAT WOULD A HORSE ORDER IN A RESTAURANT?

Not a hamburger. Horses are herbivores; they live on grass, hay, grains, legumes and some fruits. To know exactly what to feed a real live horse, it's best to check with a real live veterinarian. Never feed a horse without permission from its owner.

Because they're grazers, designed to take in small amounts of food over a long period of time, it's best to feed a horse several small meals during the day rather than one or two big ones. For all their size and strength, horses have surprisingly delicate tummies. If a horse over-eats, he can't fix it the way you can; horses can't throw up! This means that a stomachache can be fatal and digestive upsets, called colic, are taken very seriously.

Having your horse wormed regularly by a veterinarian is also crucial for his digestive health.

Basic Horse Care

If you are truly horse crazy, you've thought of having a horse live in your bedroom. It never works. Given their choice, horses would prefer to live outdoors all the time. Of course, an adequate source of fresh water is essential and they need shade from sun and shelter from rain and snow. If your horse is physically active, he might need some hay or feed and a mineral block to lick but, basically, horses can thrive on good pasture grass. Horses confined to stalls must have time for "just being a horse." This means you need to turn them out daily in a corral big enough for them to roll on their backs and run around. If horses are kept confined for too long, they can become ill. Free time is also good for his mental health.

The Bare Essentials

ter 🌿 Shelter 🌿 Food 🌿 Fresh air
Room to run 🌿 Buddies
Hugs and pats

You've heard that horses sleep standing up. It's true that horses take naps on their feet thanks to the ability to lock their legs in a standing position. But for some real z's, horses lie down. Straw or wood shavings make good bedding for horses. They provide warmth and absorb moisture.

For housekeeping, you will need to muck out his living space twice a day. This means picking up the manure with a manure fork then scooping up the wet bedding with a shovel and replacing it with fresh bedding.

Each day you must also be sure your horse has enough fresh, clean water available to him.

Remember, horses like living in herds; they are very social animals and seek companionship. If you can't have two horses, how about a goat, donkey or even a barn cat to be your horse's pal? He'll be happier with friends. Aren't you?

Grooming

A clean horse is a happy horse — or at least a healthier horse. Here are some tools and tips for your horse's personal hygiene.

 For everyday grooming you must start with a dry horse. Begin by rubbing your horse's body (not the legs or face) with a rubber curry comb **a**. Use circular movements to loosen dirt and hair.

 Next, brush off the dirt and hair with a dandy brush (a stiff brush) **b** using quick, flicking movements.

 Follow this with long smooth strokes with a body brush (a soft brush) **c**. You can now brush the legs and face with the body brush, too.

 Pick the hooves with a hoof pick **d**, gently running the pick down each side of the frog, away from your body. Brush out the lifted dirt.

 Carefully comb through the mane and tail with a large plastic bristled brush **e**. Start at the bottom of the tail and take your time with the tangles.

Bathing

Washing a horse is a little like hosing down a fidgety truck. You WILL get wet. Have someone show you how to safely tether your horse or have a friend hold him. Gently hose his whole body but don't spray water directly in his face. Once he's wet, soap him up with a big sponge and some horse shampoo. Then rinse him off and use a sweat scraper to squeegee the excess water off the main part of his body (don't use the scraper on his legs or face). Use a wet towel to clean his face, ears and nostrils. Towel him down all over and walk him around until he's dry.

sweat scraper

Types and Breeds

There are hundreds of horse breeds from all over the world. Breeds are grouped into types. Here you'll learn the different types and the popular breeds in each type.

Types

Ponies
Small breeds standing under 14.2-hands high.

Light breeds
Weigh less than 1300 pounds (585 kg.) This is the type you see most often as riding horses.

Heavy or draft breeds
Weigh up to 3000 pounds (1350 kg) with large bones and sturdy legs. They were originally bred for pulling and hauling work.

Warmbloods
A blend of draught horse and a light breed. Popular as jumpers.

Miniature Horses
Tiny breeds that can be as small as 6 hands high. although too small to ride, they can pull an adult in a cart. They have also been successfully trained as "seeing eye" animals.

I'm a Dutch Warmblood. Other Warmblood breeds include Hanoverian, Friesian, Trakehner and Selle Francais.

I'm a Pony of the Americas. Other pony breeds include Shetland, Connemara, Welsh and Chincoteaque.

I'm a toy horse.

I'm a **Quarter Horse.**
Other light breeds include
Thoroughbred, Arabian,
Saddlebred, Morgan
and Appaloosa

Breeds

I'm a **Clydesdale.**
Other draft breeds
include Shire, Percheron,
Suffolk Punch and Belgian.

I'm a **Miniature Horse.** Miniature breeds
include Falabella and
Australian Miniature, as
well as mini versions of
pony and horse breeds.

31

Gaits

gait \gāt\ *n* 1: manner of moving on foot
2: a particular pattern or style of such moving

All horses have four basic gaits:

1 Walk

Each foot strikes the ground individually in a 4-beat gait.

2 Trot or jog

Diagonal pairs of feet strike the ground at the same time in a 2-beat gait. Standardbred trot racers can also pace — a trot where the legs on each side move together in the 2-beat gait.

3 Canter or lope

A front foot strikes first, then the opposite front foot and it's diagonal hind foot hit the ground simultaneously followed by the final hind foot in a 3-beat gait.

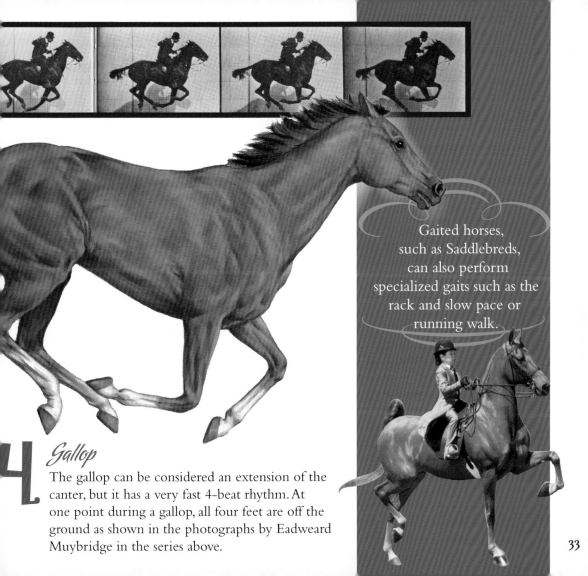

Gaited horses, such as Saddlebreds, can also perform specialized gaits such as the rack and slow pace or running walk.

4 Gallop

The gallop can be considered an extension of the canter, but it has a very fast 4-beat rhythm. At one point during a gallop, all four feet are off the ground as shown in the photographs by Eadweard Muybridge in the series above.

Riding Styles

There are many riding styles but the two big categories are Western and English.

Western

Western riding started in the American West. It's the style you see cowboys ride. It's used for reining, barrel racing and other rodeo events. Western saddles have a distinctive horn in the front used in roping (also good for hanging onto!) The saddle is deep and wide and rises high in front and in back of the rider. Riders keep their stirrups long and take a comfy backward-leaning posture in that big ol' easy chair of a saddle. They ride with their reins loose and held in one hand (to leave the other hand free for roping). They use "neck reining," pressing the rein against the neck of the horse to steer. Western bridles are very simply constructed but can be quite ornate with stamped leather and silver accents.

Western tack

"Tack" means saddles, bridles and related equipment you use with your horse. You should clean your tack after each ride. Wipe it down with a dryish damp sponge or cloth. Every week clean the leather with a glycerine saddle soap or other leather conditioner/cleaner. This also gives you a chance to check for wear and tear.

bridle

saddle

cinch

THE GOAL OF ALL
RIDING DISCIPLINES
IS A BALANCED RIDE
WITH A BALANCED
HORSE

English

There are three types of English riding: Hunt Seat, Saddle Seat and Dressage. If you want to learn English riding, Hunt Seat is a good place to start.

Hunt Seat is from the English fox hunting field and involves jumping over obstacles. With Hunt Seat riders keep their balance more forward than with Western. The saddle's seat is relatively shallow, and there's no horn on the front. Hunt Seat riders use shorter stirrups than in other disciplines so that they can lift off their horse's back over jumps. In English riding the rider holds the reins in two hands and keeps them short enough to feel contact with the horse's mouth. English bridle construction is a bit more complex than with a Western bridle but it has little or no ornamentation.

Hunt Seat Tack

bridle

saddle

girth

Saddle Seat

Saddle Seat has its roots in the American South and uses gaited horses such as Tennessee Walkers or Saddlebreds. These breeds are known for flashy, high-stepping action and can have five gaits. In addition to the walk, trot and canter, five-gaited horses also perform the slow gait and rack. The saddle is very flat and the rider sits far back on the horse. This allows for the horse's shoulders to move freely and his legs to step very high. Horses are ridden in a double bridle which has two bits and double reins.

CHAMPION

Dressage

Dressage developed from military training to a highly disciplined form of competition. Horses and riders are brought along through a series of training levels to execute complex movements. Dressage is performed in a low-fenced court with letters marking points where a particular movement is to begin or end. The saddle has a deep seat and longer flaps than in other English disciplines. Double or full bridles are used for upper-level Dressage.

Safety & Equipment

Horses are large, unpredictable creatures. Although it is not in their nature to willingly harm humans, it's possible to get hurt around them. Of course, falling off is one way to get some bruises, but to avoid anything more serious **it is REQUIRED that you always wear a Safety Equipment Institute-approved riding helmet when mounted.** Helmets designed for other purposes (cycling, skating, etc.) are not adequate for horseback use.

Always wear an SEI-approved riding helmet.

Proper footwear is the next most important piece. You need a hard-soled boot with at least a one inch heel. The heel can keep your foot from slipping through your stirrup and getting caught in the event of a fall. Good saddles have safety bars that allow the stirrup leather to slide free if a rider is dragged. There are also safety stirrups with elastic bands that pop loose if a foot gets caught.

Long pants such as jeans or riding pants are the best choice for riding. Chaps worn over pants add comfort and help prevent chaffing. The exact clothing you'll need will depend on the riding style you choose and your experience level. Ask for help at a good riding shop.

Riding gloves are not critical but they protect your hands and give you a better grip on your reins. Always a good thing!

Another important safety tip: **Keep your equipment in good working order.** Saddle and bridle leather can fail if it's allowed to dry out. Keep your tack clean and conditioned and go over it once a week to check for cracks or weak spots. Do the same with all equipment.

It's worthwhile to invest some money in your helmet and tack. Buy good quality equipment and take good care of it.

Horse Handling

The training and handling of horses is rooted in military history. The tradition of mounting and dismounting on the left side started because soldiers had their swords on the left side and could more easily swing their right leg over the horse.

Riders still mount and dismount from the left side today. We lead horses from the left side and put on saddles and bridles from the left side. Almost all horses are still trained this way. So always work with a new horse from his left side until you get to know him.

We mentioned that horses' eyes can see almost 360 degrees around. Their blind spots are directly in front and directly behind. This means it's a good idea to approach a horse at an angle so that he can see you as you come up to him. If you need to go behind a horse, approach his side and pat him as you walk closely behind his rump. If you stay close, you won't get the full impact if he kicks. Or you can pass far enough away that you're out of kicking range all together. Never goof around right behind a horse — a kick is no joke.

Do not let dogs or kids (or grown-ups) run wild around horses. Many horses don't feel comfortable around noisy, scurrying creatures. Again, a kick can cause serious injury.

To be safe around horses keep your mind on your horse and be aware of your surroundings. Wear the appropriate safety gear and keep your equipment in good condition. You'll both be fine.

Making Mini Tack

Your Klutz horse will need a wardrobe. We've enclosed the materials you'll need to make an English Hunt Seat saddle, a bridle and a blanket.

The saddle

2 stirrups

stirrup leather

girth

saddle leather

stencil for saddle pieces

glue

You will also need:
ballpoint pen
scissors

Tack Glue

1 The saddle leather has a rough side and a smooth side. Lay the leather on a table with the rough side facing up.

smooth

rough

You want the rough side up.

main saddle piece

seat piece

panel piece

2 Lay the stencil on top of the saddle leather. With a ballpoint pen, trace the three saddle pieces onto the leather.

3 Cut out each of the saddle pieces. Use short little cuts and try not to pull the leather too much with each snip.

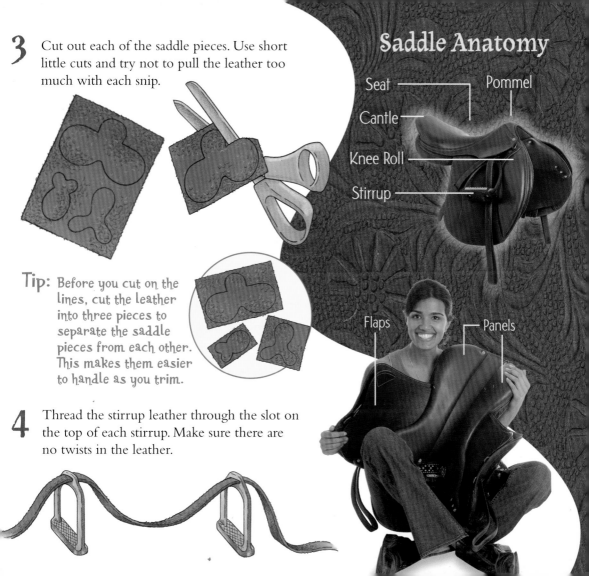

Tip: Before you cut on the lines, cut the leather into three pieces to separate the saddle pieces from each other. This makes them easier to handle as you trim.

4 Thread the stirrup leather through the slot on the top of each stirrup. Make sure there are no twists in the leather.

Saddle Anatomy

Seat

Pommel

Cantle

Knee Roll

Stirrup

Flaps

Panels

5 Now lay your stirrup pieces right on top of our picture to create a triangle. It's important that the sections of leather are the same length as in the picture.

Make sure the leather ends come up from the bottom of the stirrup slots as shown.

6 Put a dot of glue in the center of the bottom edge of your triangle.

7 Pull down the leather from the left side and lay it on top of the bottom edge. Press it into the dot of glue and gently pull the end of the strip down a little as shown.

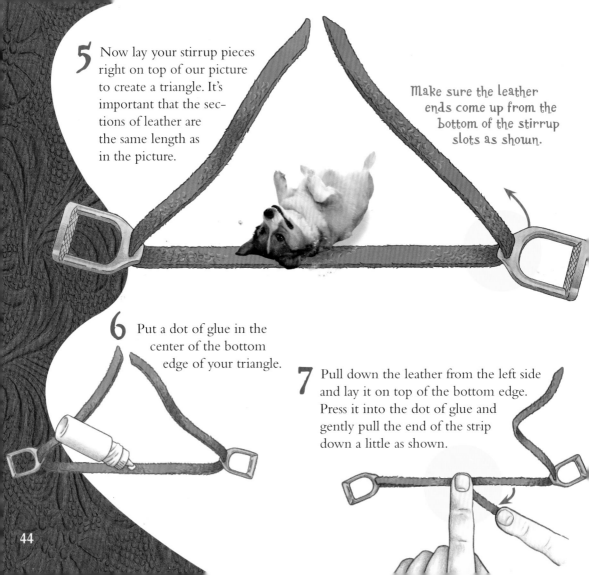

8 Put another dot of glue directly over where the first dot went but on this new leather piece.

11 Center the stirrup leather on the dot of glue. The stirrups should run across the widest part of the main saddle piece.

9 Pull down the leather from the right side and lay it on top of the other pieces. Press it into the glue, then pull the leftover end down slightly. Your stirrups should look like the pictue below, with the three pieces of leather glued together in the center.

12 Next, cover the rough side of the seat piece with a thin layer of glue.

rough side up

10 Now lay the main saddle piece on the table with the smooth side facing up. Place a dot of glue on the piece **right here.**

smooth side up

13 Lay the seat piece on top of the stirrup leather and main saddle piece, lining up at the cantle.

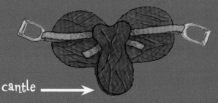

cantle ➙

14 Press the layers together. If a little glue squishes out the edges just wipe it off with your finger.

Let your saddle dry for about 15 minutes before continuing.

15 Turn your saddle over so that the stirrups are resting on the table and the rough side of the main saddle piece is facing up. The cantle should be closest to you.

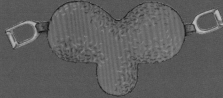

16 Now find your girth. With the buckle on the left side, lay it upside down on the main saddle piece. Check the buckle in our picture to see if your girth is laid down correctly.

girth

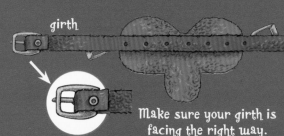

Make sure your girth is facing the right way.

17 Put some glue on the main saddle piece where shown in our picture. Use small dots of glue and — very important! — don't get glue on the girth.

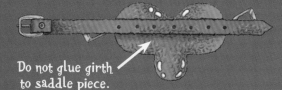

Do not glue girth to saddle piece.

18 Lay the panel piece, smooth side up, over the girth and on the main saddle piece, lining them up at the cantle.

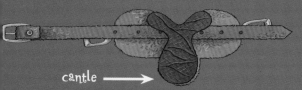

cantle ➞

19 Let the glue dry for at least 30 minutes. Then place the saddle on your Klutz horse — cantle at the rear! Wrap the long end of the girth under his belly and buckle it under the flap on the left side of the saddle.

The Bridle

To make your bridle, you start with four leather strips of different lengths. Lay out your leather strips right on top of our picture so you know which piece is which.

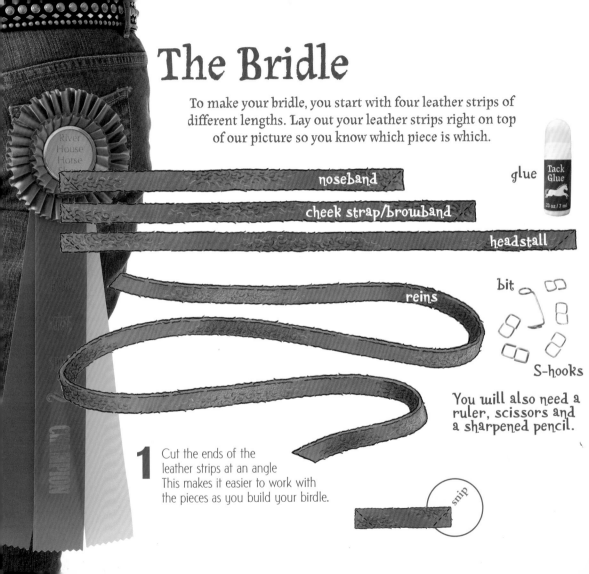

glue

noseband

cheek strap/brouband

headstall

reins

bit

S-hooks

You will also need a ruler, scissors and a sharpened pencil.

1 Cut the ends of the leather strips at an angle This makes it easier to work with the pieces as you build your birdle.

snip

2 Lace an S-hook onto one end of the **noseband** then lay the noseband down on a table. Look at our picture to make sure your S-hook is facing the right way.

3/4" (1.75 cm)

backside of S-hook

Place a dot of glue on the leather as shown.

Fold the short leather end over the S-hook to form a loop. Press the pieces together.

3 Repeat step 2 to attach an S-hook to one end of the **cheek strap/browband** piece. Set aside your noseband and cheek strap/browband pieces for now.

4 Lace two S-hooks onto the **headstall** piece. Center the two hooks on the leather and adjust them so that they are about 3/4" (1.75 cm) apart.

3/4" (1.75 cm)

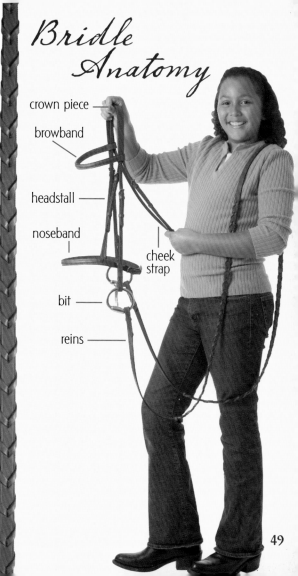

Bridle Anatomy

crown piece
browband
headstall
noseband
cheek strap
bit
reins

5 Loop one end of the **reins** through a ring on the bit. Glue it down as you did with the noseband and cheek strap/browband. Make sure there are no twists in the reins, and then loop the other end of the reins through the other bit ring. Glue it down, too.

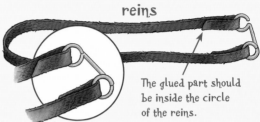

reins

The glued part should be inside the circle of the reins.

6 Look at our picture and lay your reins, bit and headstall on the table the same way. Make sure the headstall S-hooks are facing the correct way.

reins   headstall

check your S-hooks

The main part of the bit should lie on the table.

7 Loop one end of the headstall through the bit ring near it. Pull the leather end up about ¼" (0.625 cm) toward the S-hook and then glue it down.

Pull the strap up — then glue.

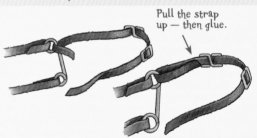

8 Loop the other end of the headstall leather up to the S-hook but DON'T GLUE IT DOWN YET.

glued

loose

The main part of the bit should lie on the table.

9 Now, go get your Klutz horse so we can custom fit his bridle.

Place the reins over your horse's neck and gently put the bit in his mouth. Ease the headstall over his ears. It's ok to stretch the leather a bit and let the unglued end of the headstall move around.

Once the bridle is over your horse's ears, pull up on the unglued headstall end until the bit rests loosely in the middle of his mouth. Hold the unglued end in place and gently take off the bridle. Lay the bridle on the table and glue down the loose end at the place you measured. Snip off any extra leather.

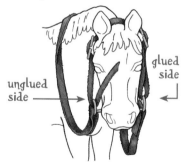

unglued side →

glued side ←

10 Now, look at this picture and lay out your bridle the same way.

11 Find your **noseband** — it's the shorter strip of leather that you set aside earlier. Hold onto the end with the S-hook. Thread the other end down through the near-side loop in the headstall and then up through the far-side loop.

Check that your noseband looks like this.

12 Now, back to your horse. Place the reins over your horse's neck and gently put the bit in his mouth. Again, ease the headstall over his ears.

13 Buckle the noseband and adjust it so that the buckle lands behind your horse's chin. Trim off all but ½" (1.25 cm) of the extra leather.

leave ½" (1.25 cm)

14 Locate the S-hook on the left side of your horse's headstall. Poke the end of a sharpened pencil under the leather at the top of the S-hook — you need to make enough room to thread your cheek strap/browband through.

Hmmm…
not all bridles
have nosebands.
If you want to
simplify your bridle,
you can leave that
part out.

15 Find your **cheek strap/browband** and thread the S-hook through the poked-out part of the headstall. Loop the leather around your horse's forehead and then through the other headstall S-hook. You might have to loosen that side with the pencil, too.

16 Move the cheek strap/browband around so that the buckle is against your horse's left cheek when you buckle it up. Look at our picture to see what we mean.

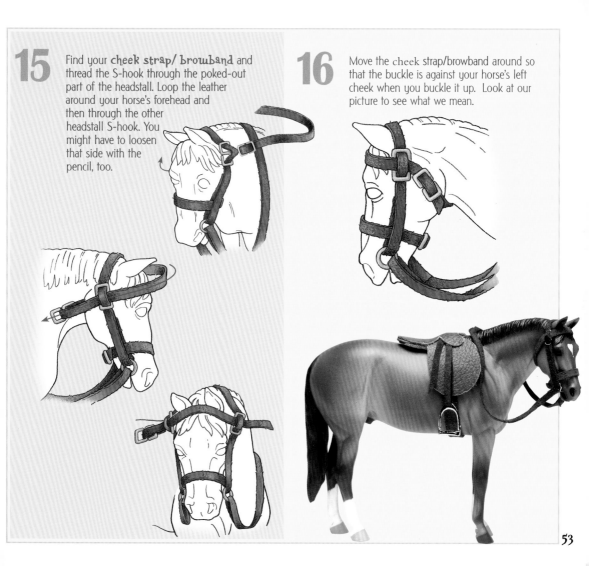

53

The Blanket

You will also need a ruler, scissors, and a pen.

1. Cut off a 1" (2.5 cm) piece of white trim. Put a bit of glue on the cut edge to keep it from unraveling. Do this on the longer piece of trim, too.

2. Lay the felt on a table and place the blanket template on top. Trace around the edges of the template with a dark pen and then cut out the shape.

3. Glue the small piece of trim to the felt where shown in our picture.

4. Flip the felt over so the trim is in the back, and then fold the felt in half — top to bottom.

5. Pull the little trim piece over and glue to the other side of the felt. Look at our picture to see what we mean.

6. Thread the longer piece of white trim through the T-shaped clip. Loop it around the clip and then glue it down.

glue here

1/2" (1.25 cm)

7 Thread the other end of the trim through the hook-shaped clip. Look at our picture to make sure your trim and clip are going the correct way. Move the hook-shaped clip so that it is 7" (17.5 cm) away from the T-shaped clip. Without moving the clip, loop the trim around the clip and glue it into place.

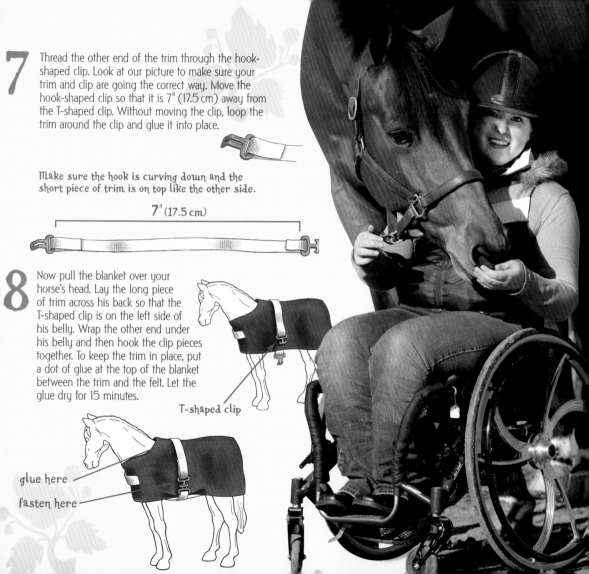

Make sure the hook is curving down and the short piece of trim is on top like the other side.

7" (17.5 cm)

8 Now pull the blanket over your horse's head. Lay the long piece of trim across his back so that the T-shaped clip is on the left side of his belly. Wrap the other end under his belly and then hook the clip pieces together. To keep the trim in place, put a dot of glue at the top of the blanket between the trim and the felt. Let the glue dry for 15 minutes.

T-shaped clip

glue here

fasten here

There is something about the beauty of horses that has inspired humankind to capture them in art for about 20,000 years. From the pre-historic cave paintings of France to modern equine artists, the horse has been a favorite subject of painters and sculptors alike.

At this very minute thousands of class notebooks are out there with doodles of horses in the margins.

How do you start to draw a horse?

It can be a bit tricky, but if you break it down into some basic shapes and proportions, you can come out with a darn good semblance of horseness.

If you can sign your name, you can draw. And even that is not a hard and fast rule.

What you need:

pencil
paper
the next few pages of this book

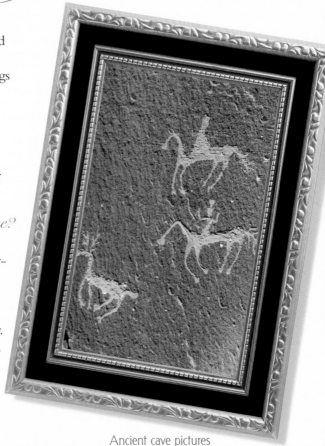

Ancient cave pictures showing people riding horses

We'll start with a horse head using some simple circles. Sketch lightly. We'll darken in later to create dimension. Tracing is allowed!

1. Draw a circle. It doesn't have to be perfect. Now add two tapered lines for your horse's nose.

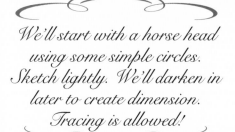

2. Add a small circle at the end of the tapered lines. This is your horse's muzzle. Add two curved lines for your horse's neck.

3. To mark where the eyes will be, imagine that your big circle is a clock face. Draw a clock hand pointing to 2 o'clock. Above 12 o'clock, draw the ears like two curvy arrows.

4. Put an almond-shaped eye at the center end of the clock hand. Make a tiny little bump at the far end for his other eye. Once the eyes are in place, you can erase the clock hand.

5. In the small circle, add a nostril that looks a little like a 6, and draw a mouth line.

6. Draw a little hotdog shape inside your horse's eyeball and color it in. Draw a circle around it for the rest of the pupil.

You can add some whisps of the mane now. Continue to add mane hairs one at a time for a really great mane.

7. Erase the simple circles and begin shading in all over. Check the horse at the right for where to lighten and darken.

8. Remember to keep a little white spot on the eyeball to show a sparkle in the horse's eyes.

An eraser is a great tool to help create highlights. Use it where you want lighter spots.

1. Draw circles for the hips and shoulders. Add lines between the circles for his tummy and back. Add the neck lines running up from the shoulders.

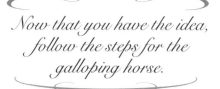

2. Add your head and muzzle circles and nose lines. You can add your ears and start your mane and tail, too.

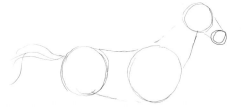

3. It starts to get tricky here. Draw in the top part of your leg lines — notice how the back leg is shaped.

4. Use little circles for the knee and ankle joints. Connect them with leg lines. Notice how the back legs bend in the opposite direction from the front legs.

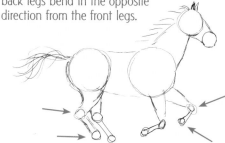

5. Add connecting lines to the hooves and then draw your hooves. Notice that the hoof shape is almost triangular.

6. Lightly shade in all over and then darken and lighten to give your horse dimension. See our horse for ideas on shading and highlighting.

61

Now put all your knowledge together to draw a rearing horse.

Your Dream Horse

Whether you have your own real live horse yet or not, you can always daydream about horses. Here's a page where you can write down all your daydreams and hopes for that special horse who has yet to enter your life, or the wonderful horse that is already here. You can create a whole life story for your Klutz horse, too. He needs a name and family tree at least!

Sire

Sire

Dam

My Horse's Name:

Sire

Dam

Dam

Date Foaled:

Place of Birth:

Breed:

Height:

Color:

What my horse does best.

How my horse greets me.

My horse's best feature.

How I found my horse.

My favorite thing to do with my horse.

My horse's favorite treat.

My horse's best friend.

My horse's favorite kind of weather.

How my horse shows happiness.

How my horse shows sadness.

How my horse likes to play.

My horse's worst habit.

The nicest thing my horse ever did for me.

The nicest thing I ever did for my horse.

A time my horse made me really proud.

An embarassing moment with my horse.

Where my horse will live when he's too old to be ridden anymore.

Write a life story for your horse. Use the ideas here to get you started.

Development & Book Design
Cornelia Thompson

Model Horse Sculpture
Stacey Tumlinson

Horse Guru
John Charlebois

Production Editor
Jennifer Mills

Production
Patty Morris

Art Direction
Kate Paddock
Jill Turney

Photography
Mark Muntean
Peter Fox
Dick Waters
Jim Naismith
Sara Leith-Tanous

Package Art
Elina Hjuberger

Giddyup Guy
John Cassidy

Drawing Horses Art
Liz Hutnick

Technical Art
Barbara Ball

Illustrations
Greg Copeland
Darwen Hennings
Jolyn Montgomery

Title Calligraphy
Nancy Hopkins

Kid Artists and Testers
MacKenzie Drazan
Shelby Drazan
Anna Harris
Samantha Levy
Paige Muschott
Leah Price
Shannon Price
Skylar Price

Special thanks to John Charlebois and the gang at Charlebois Farm
(both horse and human)

Thanks also to
Sargent Greg Trapp & The San Jose Police Department Mounted Unit, Jennifer Dixon, Neda DeMayo & Return to Freedom, Starbucks, Tiedown Saddlery, Jeanne Williams & The Laurelvale Clydesdales, and Peter

People Models
Alice Adriaenssens, Anjuli Bedi, Josie Bianchi, Samantha Bishop, Petra Bullock, Hunt Burdick, Riette Burdick, Christine Burke, K.K. Clark, Stephanie Cochrane, Makaela Cooper, Keani Dame, Chris Doyle, Hallee Foster, Amy Furstman, Melanie Galindo, Michelle Gomes, Jennifer Henderson, Haley Hirschhorn, Alec Lawler, Chloe Lê Lawler, Emily Livermore, Haley Perkins, Lauren Potter, Elizabeth Rowen, Danny Schultz, McKinley Siegfried, Megan Smith, Madeline MacGregor Taylor, Molly Pope Taylor, Lila Townsend, Sheila Townsend

Horse Models
Bert, Buddy, Casanova, Diamond, Dinah, Doc, Dutch, Easy, Fendi, Flores, Generale Ariosa, Frosty, Golden, Honey, Jessica, Jessie, King, Kiss, Lee Ambra, Melody, Mikey, Oliver, Party Time, Rudy, Scruffy, Silvo, Smokey, Spartan, Spirit, Spot on Tony, Stewart, Ticket, Webster, Wiki

Dog Models
Mr. Buster Brown, Domino Fox

Get Involved with Horses

To find more ways to become involved with horses and learn how they can enrich people's lives, check out the following:

Return to Freedom
Neda DeMayo, Founder
P.O. Box 926
Lompoc, CA 93438
www.returntofreedom.org

North American Riding for the Handicapped Association
P.O. Box 33150
Denver, CO 80233
www.narha.org

United States Pony Clubs, Inc.
4041 Iron Works Parkway
Lexington, KY 40511
www.ponyclub.org

Photo Credits

Pages 6-7: Stock Connection RM Stock Photography

Pages 26-27: Brand X Pictures Stock Photography

Pages 28-29: The Image Bank/Getty Images

Page 30: Horse Stamps, The Card Ladies

Pages 32-33: Photos by Eadweard Muybridge, Dover Pictorial Archive Series 1985

Page 37: background design K&Company LLC

Pages 38-39: Over the Gate, Full Cry by Max Francis Klepper © Red Fox Fine Art Gallery

Page 58: Whistlejacket by George Stubbs © The National Gallery (London)

Page 59: PhotoDisc

Pages 60-64: Artwork from Moseman's Illustrated Guide for Purchasers of Horse Furnishing Goods

Don't forget:
You can jump without your horse,
but NEVER without your helmet!

Jump into More Great Books from Klutz

Spiral Draw   Twirled Paper
Paper Stained Glass   Picture Bracelets
Lettering in Crazy, Cool, Quirky Style   Paper Fashions
It's All About Me   Ribbon Purses
Crochet   Friendship Bracelets

Can't get enough? Here are some ways to keep the Klutz coming.

1 Order more of the supplies that came with this book at Klutz.com. It's quick, it's easy and, seriously, where else are you going to find this exact stuff?

2 Get your hands on a copy of the Klutz Catalog. To request a free copy of our mail order catalog, go to Klutz.com/catalog.

3 Become a Klutz Insider and get e-mail about new releases, special offers, contests, games, goofiness and who-knows-what-all. If you're a grown-up who wants to receive e-mail from Klutz, head to klutz.com/certified.

If any of this sounds good to you, but you don't feel like going online right now, just give us a call at 1-800-737-4123. We'd love to hear from you.